T0158887

Just
Passing
Through

From a Suicidal Mind
to a Heart of Truth

Words by Caitlin Leigh

BALBOA.
PRESS
A DIVISION OF HAY HOUSE

Balboa Press books may be ordered through booksellers or by contacting:

Balboa Press
A Division of Hay House
1663 Liberty Drive
Bloomington, IN 47403
www.balboapress.com
1 (877) 407-4847

Because of the dynamic nature of the Internet, any web addresses or links contained in this book may have changed since publication and may no longer be valid. The views expressed in this work are solely those of the author and do not necessarily reflect the views of the publisher, and the publisher hereby disclaims any responsibility for them.

The author of this book does not dispense medical advice or prescribe the use of any technique as a form of treatment for physical, emotional, or medical problems without the advice of a physician, either directly or indirectly. The intent of the author is only to offer information of a general nature to help you in your quest for emotional and spiritual well-being. In the event you use any of the information in this book for yourself, which is your constitutional right, the author and the publisher assume no responsibility for your actions.

Any people depicted in stock imagery provided by Thinkstock are models, and such images are being used for illustrative purposes only.
Certain stock imagery © Thinkstock.

Print information available on the last page.

ISBN: 978-1-5043-7587-0 (sc)
ISBN: 978-1-5043-7589-4 (hc)
ISBN: 978-1-5043-7588-7 (e)

Library of Congress Control Number: 2017903065

Balboa Press rev. date: 03/08/2017

Dedicated to: Kirsten Stople, Cameron
Sherman, and Marc Rebadow

ACKNOWLEDGEMENTS

Along my journey I have been inspired and assisted by many beautiful beings and places. I would like to begin by thanking a foreign volunteer program, as this is where my journey inward began. I would also like to thank two eating disorder facilities for assisting my sobriety and recovery towards living a healthier life and allowing me to discover my inherent beauty and writing abilities. Energy healing and Buddhism have been a great support throughout the entire process of writing this book and my life. I would love to thank my graduate school program for assisting my journey in healing and becoming a writer. I am in deep gratitude towards all of my therapists and life coaches who have held space for me to grow and flourish. Thank you to Seattle, Washington for bringing forth my creative gifts while I come beautifully undone. Lastly, I would love to thank all of my family and friends and my amazing boyfriend who have encouraged me along the way towards living a life of freedom, joy, happiness, and creativity. It is because of all of you that I was able to write this book, and it is because of all of you that I am in deep gratitude for each moment.

INTRODUCTION

I have been plagued by a society in which I must bend in order to blend. Rules and regulations are created for the sake of protection but have led to much destruction. Truth, an assiduous lover. Capricious to another. It is a novel concept that can often be misunderstood. Perhaps, it is like a forbidden fruit. It waits and waits and waits to be spoken, and waits to be heard. To be lived. Truth, is an ineffable, yet sought after topic of our world today. If not truth, it is presumed to be a lie. But what is truth, and what is a lie if there is a notable difference in how each and every person perceives? The truth is palpable. Our bones can taste it, and our soul speaks its frequency. Everything else is white noise, yet we are consumed by just this. Many yearn to live a life of truth, but are tangled in the web of self induced and monotonous suffering. We are intricately woven into the external world, abandoning within. The truth washes away into the heavy tides as we are enveloped by such suffering. How is one to return to the state of truth under such extreme conditions?

Words

Let this poetry
Pull your pain
To the surface
Sit with it
Nurture it.

Color

Waking as
Time passing by
Flickering glitter light
Rainbow iridescent night
Prodigious shadow bright
Abundant beautiful life.

Destiny

If it keeps you awake
Let it
Become your fate.

Shooting Stars

Darling
Didn't you know
That you are exquisite
As you are
Just in the way
We stare in awe
Of shooting stars.

Should

My lungs
Are like ashes
Burnt from all the times
I wish I had said
I love you.

Heal

My heart yearns
To heal your soul
My heart longs
To be whole
Your soul whispers
All it needs to know.

Void

Empty words
Lather
Her swollen mouth
Too afraid
To speak them out.

We

There is only you
That which is me
We are simply
A divine
Infinite
Galaxy.

Lonely

Surrounded
By many
Understood
By none.

Canvas

The blank canvas
Told me
Create
The life
You dream.

One

All the things I read
All the people I meet
All the experiences
Are inherent
A part of me.

Boundary

I've learned
That your yes
Is no more important
Than my no.

Greed

You
Quenched my thirst
And I
Sucked you dry
Because I
Needed the high.

Dagger

I am unable to count
The amount of times
The knife
Has comforted me
In the darkest
Of nights.

Fantasy

She's got a dark closet
Of unmet needs
Afraid that her fantasies
Are a bit too
Extreme.

Dive

Her depths
Are deeper
Than they
Are able to meet.

Abuse

I treated my body
As if it were expendable
My soul wept
And paid the price.

Questions

Your wonder
And depth
Are the solvent
To the encrusted mind
Freeing the shackles
From the psyche
That was once blind.

Limitations

To define
Is to limit.

Ask

She sedated herself
Too ashamed
To ask for help.

Devotion

I
Am worth
Living for.

Kiss

I kiss your sins
As though they are scars
But after a glimpse
I realized they are stars
With broken hearts.

Dreams

I go to sleep
Just to be with you.

Silence

Be quiet
So I can hear you
Speak.

Further

Beyond
The agony
Is a closeness
Interconnectedness
To the God
In me.

Beat

Solitude
Is the only beat
I keep rhythm to.

Depression

It is like there are two people inside and I am constantly feeling the divide. Joy tries to speak to sadness, but they just don't coincide. One will take over and the other will run and hide. When joy is around everyone has a jovial time! But if sadness stays for too long, everyone says their goodbyes. I feel the push and then the pull, somebody help me get this right. For now, I will extend gratitude for simply being alive.

Be

I waited for you
To tell me
Who I
Am supposed to be
Abandoning soul
To be something.

Unattached

Wrap yourself around me
As if
You are
To never let me go
And if you do
I would still feel
As if I am emanating
The earth's glow.

Humanity

If I had forgiven you
I would have never
Hurt myself.

Imitation

I tried to be you
But you
You were already taken.

Prison

My body
Is a prison
Contaminated
By unnerving distortions.

Greener

To understand
The only way
Is through.

Absolute

The absolute
Is revealed
Beyond certainty
On the edge of existence.

Bulimia

The only thing
Anger has done for me
Is destroy
My esophagus
Liver
And the enamel
On my teeth
Simultaneously.

Fiction

Remember
Not everything
They tell you
Is true
And your thoughts
Those are fleeting
Fictional characters too.

Overdraw

I ask the universe
To overdraw me
And give my soul
The courage
To break
Over
And over again
Until I
Am open.

Commitment

She craved solitude
To disguise
Her apathy towards commitment
As rejection
Is only plausible
In the company
Of another.

Codependency

The most powerful source of destruction—
Complacency in solitude.

Critic

I would never wish upon another
To feel my thoughts
I barely survived them.

Animate

We cling to things
Because things
Don't break your heart
Raw
Alive
Sentient beings
Those do.

Dear

Dear sins
You do not define me
I
Am no more
Or less
I became
Because of you.

Adage

Know thyself—
I
Extends beyond
Your own skin.

Die

Some die
Just to create
And they
Come alive.

Save

People will abandon themselves
Within a matter of a second
Just to be saved
By someone else
Who is seeking
The same.

Companion

Solitude
Is the only companion
Who has never
Broken my heart
Death—
A close second.

Pray

I wish to feel the world
As my soul
Dear Lord
I beg
I beg to go home.

Fluent

Love—
It speaks
Every language.

Up

I've never found a better lover
Than the stars
They continuously
And tenderly
Make love to you
Wherever you are.

Delusional

The voices
I had to tell them to stop
Telling me things
I am not.

Trespass

You
Touched me
In a way
That I will never
Allow from another.

Within

If you do not spend time alone
You will always be looking
For a place
To call home.

Eating Disorder

She was like a tyrant, a bully. Always beating me up, and pushing everyone away. So I would hide alone in my closet, filled with humiliation. And she continued berating me. Degrading my worth. That's no friend. That's no enemy. That's someone who needs help. That's someone who needs love. And so I began giving her just that. She became louder, and grew larger. Subtle shifts started to occur. She began to unravel, softening around her tough edges. And then, her edges dissipated. And she, soft.

Thin

I chased
After you
But never
Have I gotten it
Quite right.

Community

My wounds
Are the gateway
Into the light of others.

Rape

I locked the door
But they barged
Right through.

Run

And they
Run
Run
Run
Just
To feel
Numb.

Comradery

Together
We can imagine
Dream
Accomplish
Be
Anything.

Stop

Detached from the physical
To disassociate
From all the touch
That was not asked of you
Or you
Or you
And you.

Incoherent

She choked on the hands
That weaved with poison
Around her flaccid neck
Until she was no longer coherent.

Decide

Stop waiting
For someone else
To do
What it is you need
To do for you.

Ephemeral

Watch as the night sky
Sets your boundless heart ablaze
Let yourself get lost
In the midst of the maze
Where you will create
A sacred
Eternal
Space.

Body

I am
No more alive
Just because
I
Dwell
In human form.

Famished

Silence
Heals the soul
Words
Clutter
Feed the famished ego.

Space

Time and space
Are inexplicable things
Just like the dreams
I have
Of you and me.

Wise

I will find the answers
That appear not to exist
But do not ask me
If I know
I cannot answer this.

Abandon

I succumbed to vengeance
And there I was
Withering
In the depths
Of abandonment.

Insanity

I explored many
Harrowing avenues
Trying to assuage the pain
But it only perpetuated
The infamous longing
Until I went insane.

Safe

And when his hands woke me
In the ambiguity
Of the night
With him
I no longer feared
No need to run
No need to hide.

Razors

To tell you the truth
I never wanted to stop
But you told me to
Or else.

They

She kissed my light
Ever so gently
But you
You found my darkness
And still looked into my eyes
As though they were divine.

Joyous

And if I only had one photo left
I would make sure
To capture
Your contagious laugh.

Unconditional

You
Exploited
All of my weaknesses
And there you went
Loving me anyway.

Mercy

So I lay you down
And you knew better
Then to fall asleep
I let you go
In mercy
We will meet.

Fail

The scale
Has always rejected
The love for myself
Without fail.

Trust

You lied
To the womb
That bred you
But I
I still believe you.

Tame

Trauma taught me
But it did not tame me
For I am free
No matter
What I have allowed
To come in between.

Man

You loved me in innocence
And loved me in corruptness
I will look no further
For a better man.

Wanderer

His wandering eyes
Made a cunning disguise
For all that was lost inside.

Fake

I never changed
I stopped the masquerade
And all those masks
I threw them away.

Honestly

You cannot
Protect someone
From their own truth.

I Cry

Here come the ineffable tides
I cry
I cry
I cry
The stars
They are my savior
Tonight.

Mystique

Rarely
Were pieces spoken
From her tranquil mouth
We had to use our imaginations
To figure
The puzzle out.

Channel

I was given
The gift of writing
Along
With feeling
Every bit of it too.

How

I pulled my roots
To the surface
And made a concoction
Of cathartic blabber.

Hush Hush

The ego is repelled
By the words
I write
Telling me to hush
Put it back
Inside.

Soft

Like a baby's bottom
Her heart
Softened
The hardened soul.

Transparency

Never feel guilty
For speaking the truth
It's the lies
You tell yourself
That are uncouth.

Follower

I have abided
For much too long
Now
I am desperate
To play
My own song.

Generative

When he gives you
His book to read
Listen.

Alchemy

And if it was
Or wasn't poison
It was an alchemist's
Dream come true.

Share

The only distress
One will encounter
Is a love repressed.

Scream

The loudest in the room
Uttered nothing
But silence.

Transform

Gratitude
Is the essence
Of alchemy.

Private

It's as if
Her story
Had just begun
When the last word
Dripped from the tip
Of her tongue.

Hope

And whatever happens
I know
We will be together
Forever.

Sacrifice

Humility
Was the only price
I paid
And now
I am set free.

Patience

And if you only knew
How I had been
Touched
Perhaps you would
Not have been
In such a rush.

Empathy

What did I do
To not deserve
Your gentleness?

Liberation

Insanity
That is where we will meet.

Closer

I have always stood closest
To the edge
That has allowed me
To understand
The beauty
And indefiniteness
Of death.

Voices

Let them be loud
The power
Lies
Within the silence.

Self-Destruction

I wanted to do everything.

Compassion

Love
Whatever destroys you
That is your best teacher.

Transient

We are all
Just transient beings
Falling in love with
What brings
Us to our knees.

Slowly

Slow down
Way down
Slower
Easy now
Gentle
Gentle
Come along
Closer
Slowly
Be still
Still
In the silence.

Emotions

Let the lion
Out of the cage
And see what happens
When you resist
The urge to tame.

Bottom

I thank every floor
Who has held me
As I have come undone.

Know

I know nothing
This is more
Than I could
Ever imagine
Knowing.

Undone

A wounded silhouette
Tightly woven
Around her heart
Slowly
Softly
Pulling
It
Apart.

Goal

I kept no destination
In mind
And lost track
Of time.

Penetrate

He crawled
Beneath her skin
Probing
Until her wound
Started to open
Again
Again
And again.

Heart Beat

It is clear
To me
That all I need
Is a heart
And a beat
To experience
Life's greatest mystery—
Living.

Flow

Relax
Into the constriction
And watch
Your heart
Expand
Into ascension.

Write

Some call it artsy
I call it
An emotional explosion
Expressed
Constructively.

Selfish

Sometimes
I am
All I think about
I am the only
Which exists.

Touch

Some things
Many
Are better left
Untouched
But the heart
That is a must.

Imagine

The truth is revealed
When our mind
Is not concealed
By all
That is unreal.

Fragmented

I am experiencing
What I perceive
A fragment
Of the truth
Of this totality.

Enough

You
Are not defined
By someone else's
Lack.

Leave

She gave me
Everything and more
But I still tried
To sneak out
The back door.

Pure

Whatever
You be
Say
Or do
May it bring
Out the God
Within
You.

Quit

Let me run
Before I fail.

Freedom

I touched
And did not keep
For nothing perishes
When free.

South

Too much to feel
And it was never
Even real.

Twin Flames

And the two
Came undone
So as to fuse
Into one.

Judge

You called me dirty
And forgot
To wash your hands.

Busy

The mind is kept occupied
Locked in overdrive
So as not to be
Left behind.

Destruction

She went on
Vandalizing
Her body
Like a vacant
Piece of property.

Self

We long for unity
And approach
With an I and me
Mentality.

Candle

I burn for you
As you light me
Up.

Hard

She wasn't hardened
She was precisely wrapped.

Sorry

I hurt you
I hurt you
I hurt you
Because I didn't know how
To stop hurting myself.

Desperate

I wasn't for sale
Even though
I still
Took everything
Without fail.

Voice

Scream louder
I am tired
Of hearing
My own.

Blend

I bend
I break
I bow
And I still breathe.

Cave

I cave
I carve
I cry
I am not afraid to die
I am ready
I am ready
To fly.

Rigid

I felt
I fell
I failed
My heart became stale.

Escapism

Endlessly searching
For an identity that will
Allow me to escape
Me.

Shame

A knife
A gun
A blade
All one in the same
An unattended device
Becomes a weapon
To a driver
Who wishes to relieve
The formidable shame.

Try

Never feel the need
To keep up
With someone else's insecurities.

True Colors

See me in red
See me in white
See me in purple
See me in yellow
See me in orange
See me in green
See me in blue
See me in the darkest of hues
But do not bequeath me
Because you saw all of me
In you.

ED

I binged
Until I cringed
Threw up
And repeated the cycle
Again and again
After I went numb
I covered my heart
With my frazzled
Yet willing hand
And vowed
To try and love myself
Again.

Take

Emptiness is at stake
When all we do
Is take
Take
And take.

Dare

They told me
Dare to dream
I honored my soul
And dared to be.

Confidence

I think, I think, I think it all the way through. Dithering in doubt, fumbling on worries of a choice yet to be made or a mistake that has not taken place. For each choice or mistake will have a ripple, so I must think it all the way through. And if I think about it enough, I'll lose my mind and not know what to do. I'll abandon these thoughts and see where the choices or mistakes lead me to. You see water, it moves however it moves. And some days it is heavy, some days soft. But water, it is strong, for it does not think, nor does it pretend to be something it is not.

Alone

Jealousy screamed
In my face
It didn't want to be left
Abandoned
Alone
Empty.

Another

I played to their weakness
And never found
My potential.

Explore

Don't get trapped
In there
Get lost
Out there!

Poise

Go in
And go out
Leave behind
Doubt.

Create

I am a creation
Created by creation
Endlessly creating.

Choice

Weapons aren't dangerous
Thoughts
Those are.

Flight

I wanted to escape life
Before the illusion
Escaped from I.

Pieces

I didn't leave them
I broke them
And was left
Broken.

Enjoy

Life is a blink
Of an eye
One moment
You are born
The next you
Are preparing
For some
Momentary goodbye.

Ours

What's mine is yours
Yours mine
We are truly connected
All the time.

Divinity

The essence of time
Flickering moments
Floating through the divine.

Norway

I feel you in my arms
I feel you in my feet
I feel you in my palms
I feel you in my knees
I feel you in my heart
You keep it soft
As the beat continues on so eloquently.

Tell

Everyone has a story
Some like to hold
Some wish to let go
But your story
Is meant to be told.

Purpose

I didn't want
Nor did I want
To be wanted
I need
I need
To to be needed.

Light Being

Layer by layer
Piece by piece
The body begins to unravel
Discretely
Light
Light
Lighter
On the feet
Heart is full
Mind
Empty
Surrendering to become
Being
Be.

Wholeness

I was never looking for you
I was looking for that part
Of me
That I left
With you.

No

Touch me here
Touch me there
Your touch
Has felt the innocence
Of my skin
The beginning
Of my wounds
The depth
Of my suffering
Please stop
I've already been touched
Everywhere.

Seen

I see you
I see me
I see color
So vividly.

Oneness

If I am you
You
Me
All is one
All is everything.

Truth

The truest of truths
Do not require the approval
Of another.

Confinement

These walls
I am confined
These walls
Protect
But do not define
These walls
Crumble
And fall
These walls
Are an illusion
Time to reveal all.

Bloom

Like a flower
Of the wild
She bloomed
Inconspicuously
Not too late
Or too soon.

Vulnerable

And they
Put their masks on
Demanding
That you must not
See their ugly.

Copies

We are meant
To create
We get sick
Because
We try to replicate.

Waves

    Each
    Is not one
    But of
    The all.

Where

Where was I
When you
Were in me
Isn't consent
Needed
For such a thing?

Extraordinary

Remind me
That all
Is temporary
This body
I inhabit
Is for
Just this
Precious moment
The animate
Inanimate
Fleeting
Specks
Of an extraordinary
Inestimable
Existence
Beyond
Imagination.

Belong

A tale once told
I belong
I am
Whole.

Open

I am
Brokenly open.

Ebulliently

A cord
Of ebullience
Sings
From the center
Of my heart
It will endure
All
Even
When it has
Been broken
Apart.

Together

To help one
Is to help
All.

Everlasting

And when on your knees
Make a vow
To the God in we
Bestowing
The gift
Of eternity.

Fans

And always
Strive together
Not only
Through the fairest
Of weather.

Meaning

Give meaning
By giving
Up seeking a meaning
And simply
Being.

Cues

Suffer
In the suffering
Or listen
And be set free.

Perception

Suffering
Suffer
Suffer
If you must
Always keep the faith
And have
A pocket full of trust.

Reveal

But what is hidden
Always comes to light
The demons
The darkness
The lies
Let them all wander outside
When heard
They will shine
Just as bright
As bright as the truth
Emanating from your eyes.

Marveling

Marvel
In the uncertainty
For it is here
That all
Is possible
Of anything.

Failure

I am not
Afraid
To live the truth
I am afraid
To disappoint
All of you.

Whole

Thee
Is in me
And you
And they
And we
Thee
Is innate
Look
Within
It is never
Too late.

Resistance

The truth is
Everything
That repels
You
Pulls you
Closer
To all
That is you.

Effortless

And some
Will eloquently
Move through
The mysteriousness
Of that
Which is deemed
Life
But death
Is simply as uncertain
For we not know
What
Is to come next.

New

I climbed
Out of
That same
Old story
Entered
A blank new page
Where
Then
I could
Endlessly
Create.

Story

I am of this
I am not
In this.

Equality

I'd like to believe
There is nothing
Superior
Or inferior
To me.

Salty

Pour thy salt
Lick thy wound
Emotions
Surface
But never
Too soon.

Self-Love

So many
I love you's
But not one
To the self.

Perfection

What is freedom
When
Rules
Are followed
By punishment
If not perfected.

Win

Take a risk
Who cares
About the fall
It's everything
In between
Not about winning
Them all.

Flaws

I found
All your wrongs
But I never
Felt right.

Defineless

We seek meaning
To find meaning
But it cannot
Be defined
Or limited
To meaning.

Harsh

These thoughts
Are exhaustible
Impossible
Creating a system
In which
I
Am unable
To coexist with.

Healer

You are
The healer
Of healers
Who heals
All.

Human

I am befuddled
By the contraption
In which
I reside
This body
Is not a device
Perhaps a conduit
Guiding
To all treasures
Yearning to speak
And be felt
So as to come alive
And never again
To be found in demise.

Key

No one
Can take
Power
From you
But you
And
Only
You.

Beauty

Hush now
Wipe the tears
Face the broken
Shadow
Empty of fear
For this entire
World
Is simply
A reflection
Of you
My dear.

Passive

Swept under
A rug
Your heart
Will always
Feel the tug.

Receptivity

I don't know
What I want
And I'm not sure
What I need
As I'm not
Used to asking
For such a thing.

Limitless

Brains
Are encumbered
By the box
Enclosed
By perpetual
Thoughts
But never
Was it locked.

Fear

A dear friend
Who reminds me
Of all the ways
In which
I am able
Yet afraid to bend
But this
I can no longer
Comprehend
As fear
Sifts through my bones
Courage
Opens its tethered hands.

Possible

There are far
Greater things
From what
Are visible to me
And I believe
They
Are not out of reach.

Spacious

Green and yellow
Burning red
I am enveloped
By the vividness
Crisp air
Streams of change
I am no more
Or less
I am
Spaciousness.

Red

Red paint
Dribbled
To the floor
My eyes stained
As I look again
Once more
This
Cannot be ignored
Help
Someone help
Her heart is broken
Shattered
Torn.

Stay

Speak up
They say
But if I do
They will be deadly afraid
Speak up
They say
While they keep talking
I'll save my tongue
For a better day
Speak up
They say
Telling me to hush
It will all be ok
Speak up
But when I do
They never stay.

Unknown

See above
Feel below
That is where
It all grows
Uncertainty
Intertwined
With hope
Make for a daring
Adventure
Into the unknown.

Ignore

Going on
And on
And on
The conditioning
Builds
Layers
Until you've buried
The trauma.

Quiet

Muffled mouth
Don't speak
The truth
May come out.

Spontaneous

There is a sense
Of ease
When you are
No longer
Confined
By the materialistic
Expectations
Deemed
Appropriate
In our society.

Absorb

Your pain
Has resorted
In me
Punishing
Myself.

Empty

I tried
And tried
And tried
To be
All that you asked of me
It was never enough
But I didn't give up
My heart severed
And now
I am finding my way
Back to love.

Material

There is no truth
In tangible
Just an unwavering
Practicality
Manifested
Into materialism.

Depart

It wasn't a place
To hide
But a place
To escape
All the pretty
Little lies
And all the dirty parts
Of me
That which I
Denied.

Good

She sacrificed her best
To settle
For her good.

Awe

Captivated
By the immanent beauty
Of this life
And to be an extension
Of this majestic creation
Blows through the limitations
Of the mind.

Travel

Lavishly
Living
One
Miraculous
Miracle
Of a life.

Competition

I didn't need
To be louder
I just wanted
To be better.

Immoral

She wanted
To crawl
Out of her
Porous skin
All she could do
Was sin
Sin
Sin.

Purge

Massacre
In her throat
Murder
She spoke.

Stallion

She walks gallantly
With freedom
By her side
Joy in her heart
And grace
Grazing in her eyes
Her spirit
Knows
Now
Is always the time.

Wait

And you wait
And wait
And wait
But one day
You wonder
What you were waiting for.

She

I broke you
But not in the same way
I know this
By how
You speak her name.

Roots

We cut trees
As if
They have no roots.

Cathartic

I do not write poetry
To be pretty
I write poetry
To heal all the parts of me
That feel
Unpretty.

Permeable

Inhale
You in
Breathing your galaxies
Into my unbounded nomadic
Skin.

All

Out beyond
The edge of edges
Of limitless space
The cosmic universe
Yields
An infinite
Billowing creation
Of void.

Feelings

One day
They
Will catch up to you
And you
Will remember
Why you
Are here.

Hummingbird

Hum
To the beat
That takes
Your heart
Home.

Wisdom

The fool
In me
Is enchanted
By
Every
Darn
Little
Thing.

Sensitive

She wanted
To leave it
All behind
A tender heart
Too soft
Maybe some
Were meant
For another time.

I AM

I am not
Swayed
By the flux
Of this phenomenon
But empowered
By the realization
That I am.

Damaged Goods

Tears streamed down
Her withering body
Now doused
In red
She shut her eyes
And begged
To forget.

Grateful

I
Am simply
A passenger
Witnessing
Divinity.

Association

Stigma;
The number one
Killer.

Projection

I found
My deepest
Passions
And dreams
In all
Who I envied.

Possibilities

They told her
What to do
What to believe
And what to think
But she discovered
Anything is possible
Anything
Can be achieved.

My Love

Your love
Is an elixir
Awakening
My soul.

Still

In stillness
We can see
In stillness
We can breathe
In stillness
We are able
To receive
In stillness
We recognize
The extraordinariness
Of our being.

Shine

There's a devil inside
That begs
To see the light
I will not forbid
Him of such
Just to conceal
My pride.

Presence

She pursued pleasure
Consistently
Chasing after
The big things
Forgetting
What really mattered
Was everything
In the in between.

Forever

Run
Run run
Before
It's too late
Always finding
Solace in escape
But what if
This time
They promised
To stay?

Intrinsic

She craved
An audience
To soothe
What was
Once
But no longer
Whole
But then
She found poetry
In the magic
Of her soul.

Water

I lost all armor
And let you in
Shattered
But I am soft enough
To mend.

War

To love
Thyself
Is to forgive
Thyself.

Persistence

I've heard
A thousand no's
But all it takes
Is one
Yes.

Within

Traveling
Into the unknown
Appeared
An unrelenting shadow
Piece by piece
She found
Her way
Back home.

Anorexia

And it was never enough. It could never quite be enough. Because it could be better. It could always be better. Better. Better. Better. My enough could not amount to better. Better wanted more, for my enough never sufficed. Enough I said to better. I am enough, and there is no better. But there is I, and I am enough. As I am. I am enough, as I am.

Strength

Encourage
Vulnerability
We are meant
To be soft.

Be You

One day
I hope you realize
How beautiful
Your true
Is.

Repeat

I am enough. I am worthy. I am love. I am light. I am whole. I am brilliant. I am open. I am strong. I am beautiful. I am resilient. I am kind. I am powerful. I am intuitive. I am soft. I am compassionate. I am fearless. I am intelligent. I am abundant. I am creative. I am amazing. I am growing. I am divine. I am one with all.

AFTERWORD

I once dreamt of being a good writer. If only I could articulate all of these feelings in an eloquent manner. And then one day, this dream came true. But not in a fairy tale-like manner. In fact, I was fortunate enough to go beyond the depths of my own being to realize my true inherent gifts. My journey inward began in 2014 after being let go from a life long dream that was shattered by low self-esteem and a lack of self-love. During my journey, writing was extremely cathartic and a good outlet for my penetrative emotions. This is how *Just Passing Through* came to fruition. A lost girl looking for love who finally looked in the mirror and decided to love herself.

ABOUT THE AUTHOR

Caitlin is a recovered bulimic, anorexic, addict, and alcoholic. She is a survivor and an ED warrior. From her recovery she received the gift of writing and transformation. Caitlin is receiving her Master's in Transpersonal Psychology with an emphasis in Life Coaching and Ecopsychology. She loves energy healing, crystals, and she chants every single day. She loves camping and hiking in the greater outdoors when she is not engaged in her writing. Caitlin plans to continue writing, coaching, learning, and sharing her experiences with others!